It's A Miracle

BY BILL AND GLORIA Gaither

Illustrated by Aletha Jones

impact books

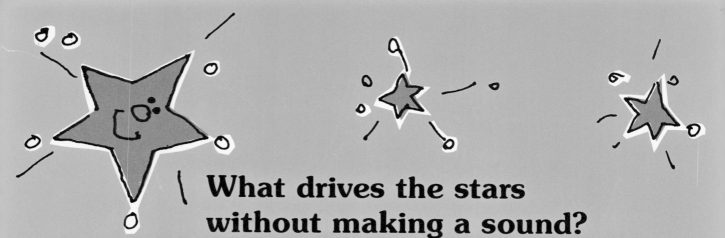

What drives the stars without making a sound?

Why don't they crash when they're spinning around?

1. What drives the stars with-out making a sound? Why don't they crash when they're spin-ning around?

2

**What holds me up
when the world's upside down?**

**I know
it's a miracle!**

D♭   B♭m

E♭m

A♭7

I Know —— It's a Miracle!

Who tells the ocean
where to stop on the sand?

What keeps the water
from drowning the land?

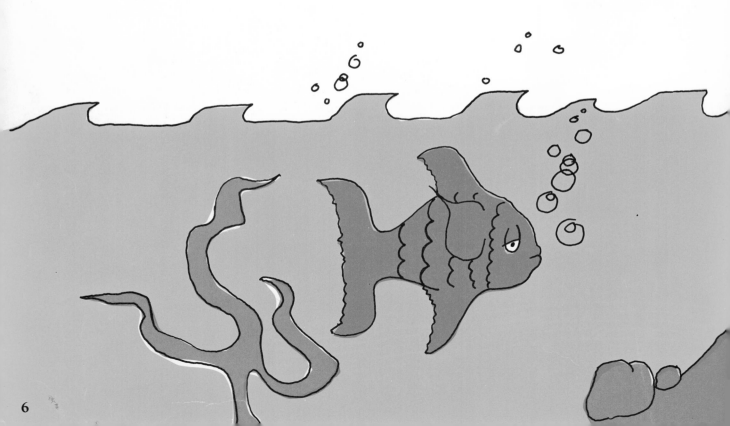

7

**Who makes the rules
I don't understand?**

**I know
it's a miracle!**

It's a miracle
just to know God is with me
wherever I go;

It's a miracle
as big as can be
that He can make a miracle of me!

A miracle of me!

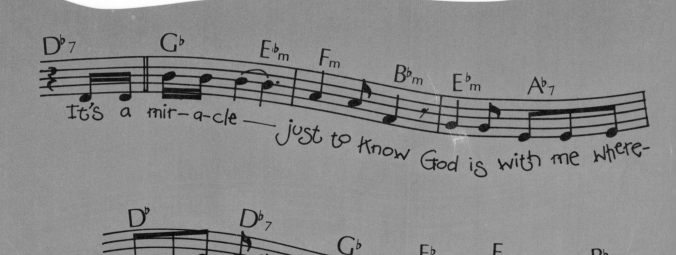

...te can make a mir-a-cle of me! A mir-a-cle of me!

12

Who shows the birds
how to build a good nest?

2. Who shows the birds how to build a good nest?

How can the geese fly so far without rest?

**Why do the ducks
go south and not west?**

**I know
it's a miracle!**

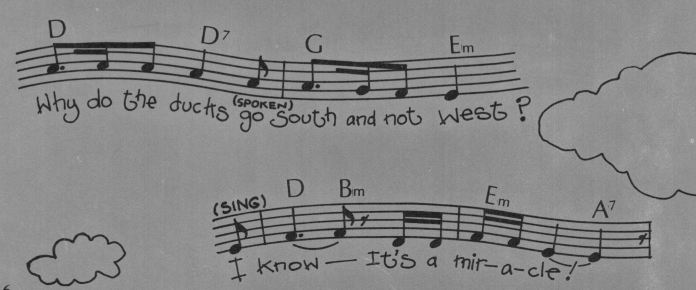

What makes a brown seed
so tiny and dry
burst into green,
grow up so high,
and shoot out blossoms of red
bye and bye?

I know
it's a miracle!

What makes a brown seed so tiny and dry

Burst in-to green, grow up so high, And

Shoot out blossoms of red bye and bye?

I know it's a mir-a-cle!

It's a miracle
just to know
that God is with me
wherever I go;

It's a miracle
as big as can be
that He can make a miracle of me!
A miracle of me!

When a spring
makes a brook
and a brook
makes a stream,

the stream makes
the river water
fresh as can be.
Who puts the salt in
when it gets to the sea?

I know
it's a miracle!

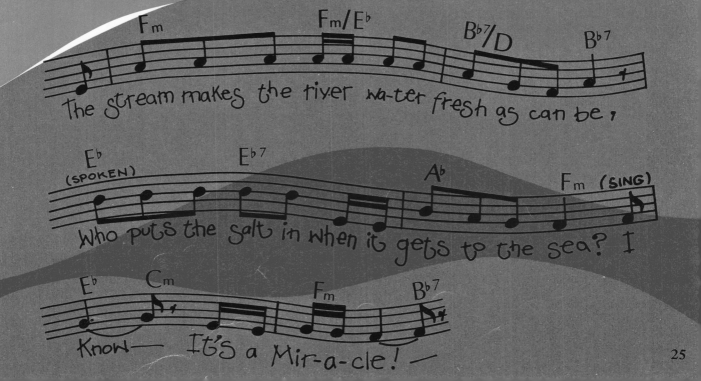

The stream makes the river wa-ter fresh as can be,

Who puts the salt in when it gets to the sea? I

Know— It's a Mir-a-cle! —

**There are thousands of people
in cities I see;**

**the world must be crowded
as crowded can be.**

**But God knows my name
and He cares about me!**

**I know,
I know,
I know
it must be a miracle!**

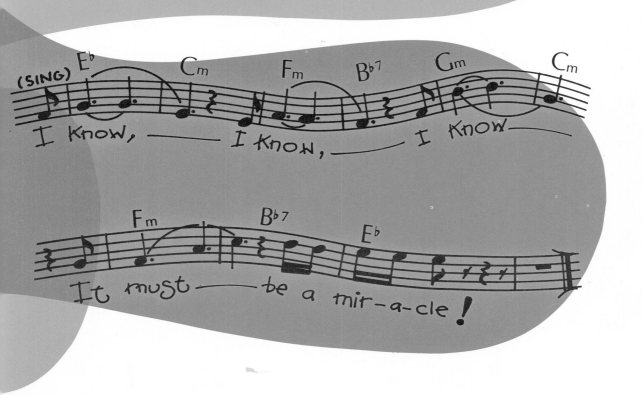